MW00954658

This Book Belongs To

Made in United States
Troutdale, OR
08/03/2023

11787034R00062